The Official White House Christmas Ornament

Collected Stories of a Holiday Tradition

The Official White House Christmas Ornament

Collected Stories of a Holiday Tradition

MARCIA M. ANDERSON

KRISTEN HUNTER MASON

THE WHITE HOUSE *HISTORICAL ASSOCIATION*

THE WHITE HOUSE HISTORICAL ASSOCIATION

VICE PRESIDENT OF PUBLICATIONS AND EXECUTIVE EDITOR Marcia Mallet Anderson
EDITORIAL AND PRODUCTION DIRECTOR Lauren McGwin
SENIOR EDITORIAL AND PRODUCTION MANAGER Kristen Hunter Mason
EDITORIAL AND PRODUCTION MANAGER Elyse Werling
EDITORIAL COORDINATOR Rebecca Durgin
CONSULTING EDITOR Ann Hofstra Grogg

SECOND EDITION
10 9 8 7 6 5 4 3 2 1

LIBRARY OF CONGRESS CONTROL NUMBER: 2021938284
ISBN: 978-1-950273-20-1

PRINTED IN ITALY

PAGE 3: DETAIL OF THE 2013 OFFICIAL WHITE HOUSE CHRISTMAS ORNAMENT, WHICH HONORS PRESIDENT WOODROW WILSON.

PAGE 5: THE 2021 CHRISTMAS ORNAMENT FEATURES A REPRODUCTION OF A PAINTING OF THE BLUE ROOM CHRISTMAS TREE THAT WAS MADE FOR PRESIDENT AND MRS. LYNDON B. JOHNSON'S 1967 CHRISTMAS CARD.

OPPOSITE: PRODUCED IN HONOR OF JAMES HOBAN, THE ARCHITECT OF THE WHITE HOUSE, THIS COMMEMORATIVE ORNAMENT IS MADE WITH STANDSTONE FROM THE AQUIA, VIRGINIA, QUARRY THAT PRODUCED THE STONE USED TO BUILD THE EXTERIOR WALLS OF THE WHITE HOUSE.

WASHINGTON, DC

Contents

Introduction

Perhaps nothing signifies the American public's affection for the White House and the presidents and first families who have lived there as does the White House Christmas Ornament. Each year for more than forty years, the White House Historical Association has produced a new ornament specially designed to commemorate a presidential administration or to mark a landmark anniversary in the history of the White House. Millions of these ornaments now decorate Christmas trees in the United States and abroad—and many have even been hung on trees in the White House itself.

The ornament program did not begin as a series, however. In 1981 the Association produced a replica of an angel from a New England weather vane, which proved an immediate and unexpected success. Word spread quickly among the federal employees in Washington, D.C., who lined up to purchase the ornament at the Association's small headquarters, and when it was featured on the *Today* show, orders came in from all over the nation. In just six weeks 4,246 ornaments were sold, generating $16,644.

Recognizing the ornament's potential, the Association planned for a 1982 ornament. Another weather vane was selected—the Dove of Peace atop George Washington's Mount Vernon. With the 1983 design featuring the North Front of the White House during the administration of President John Adams, the concept of the ornament program as an educational tool was further developed. It was determined that the ornament themes would proceed through the presidents in order, with occasional pauses in the chronological march to recognize White House anniversaries. The Board of Directors determined that, like all of the White House Historical Association's products, the ornaments must serve an "educational and interpretive purpose" and "clearly and uniquely relate to the White House." To fullfill this directive, ornaments are packaged with booklets that tell the story of the presidency honored and the events commemorated.

FIRST LADY LAURA BUSH SHOWS OFF THE OFFICIAL WHITE HOUSE CHRISTMAS ORNAMENT, IN HONOR OF PRESIDENT ANDREW JOHNSON, ON THE BLUE ROOM CHRISTMAS TREE IN DECEMBER 2001.

As the focus on historical relevency and the high-quality production values increased, sales soared. The 1983 ornament sold more than 13,000 prior to Christmas; the 1984 ornament, 26,400. The Association had to hire temporary employees to fulfill the orders. Longtime employees and customers still remember the long lines that wrapped around the block and stretched down H Street despite rain and snow. When inventory temporarily ran out, as it often did in the weeks before Christmas, determined customers often chose to wait in line until the next delivery truck arrived. The ornaments had quickly become collector's items, and many organizations placed orders in bulk often giving the ornaments as Christmas gifts to employees and clients or using them in fund-raisers. By the mid-1980s income from ornament sales was already playing a significant role in funding the Association's mission.

The designs of the ornaments are now planned far in advance and over the years they have become increasingly complex. Some ornaments are two-sided, some three-dimensional. Moving parts were introduced in 1984, and enamel colors in 1986. Some ornaments incorporate ceramic or porcelain ovals printed with paintings or portraits. The 2009 ornament features a hologram. The 2015 ornament has hidden LED lights. All the ornaments are finished with a ribbon or gold cord and since 1983 have been variously inscribed with "Christmas," the year, "The White House," and a reference to the presidential administration or White House anniversary being recog-

FIRST LADY HILLARY CLINTON DISCUSSES THE OFFICIAL WHITE HOUSE CHRISTMAS ORNAMENT IN HONOR OF PRESIDENT ZACHARY TAYLOR DURING A PRESS PREVIEW OF THE WHITE HOUSE CHRISTMAS DECORATIONS IN THE BLUE ROOM, DECEMBER 1995.

nized. Many incorporate additional special quotations and inscriptions. The first two ornaments were originally copper with a chemically patinated finish that gave a weathered look. Now reissues of those ornaments, and all subsequent ornaments, have been 24K gold-finished brass. They shine and never tarnish. The ornaments are kept continuously in stock in the Association's shops and are available year-round on the Association's website. In recent years, new ornaments are revealed each year with in a special event, often at a Presidential Library on Presidents' Day in February.

Today the White House Christmas Ornaments are a long-standing and beloved tradition. Families, businesses, and nonprofit organizations decorate their trees with them and give them as gifts. Some take pride in displaying entire sets.

The forty-first ornament, which honors President Lyndon B. Johnson, was made during the White House Historical Association's sixtieth anniversary year. It symbolizes the Association's continuing work to fulfill the vision of our founder, First Lady Jacqueline Kennedy, that the nonprofit Association would serve as a private partner in maintaining the White House while educating Americans about its history.

Gina Sherman
Vice President of Retail Strategy and Sales
The White House Historical Association

I *Angel in Flight*

The design of the White House Historical Association's first Christmas Ornament represents a traditional symbol of Christmas. It is the Angel Gabriel, who appeared to Mary to announce that she would bear a son, the Savior, and should name him Jesus. Gabriel is in flight, bearing a trumpet.

The design comes from a weather vane made in 1840 for the Universalist Church in Newburyport, Massachusetts. Cut from sheet iron by the Charlestown, Massachusetts, firm Gould & Hazlett, the Angel Gabriel sat atop the church for almost fifty years. When the church closed, the weather vane was moved to the steeple of the People's United Methodist Church, where it became a Newburyport landmark. In 1965, a watercolor of the weather vane by the artist Lucille Chabot was featured on a U.S. postage stamp, bringing it national attention. This iconic example of American folk art is now in the collection of the Smithsonian Institution, and Chabot's painting of it is in the collection of the National Gallery of Art.

As weather vanes crown many of the nation's historic buildings, including Independence Hall and Mount Vernon, the silhouetted Angel Gabriel weather vane was an appropriate choice for the White House Historical Association's Christmas Ornament. At the White House, it was hung on the Reagan administration's Blue Room Christmas tree.

MEASURING 2¼ x 4½ INCHES, THE ORIGINAL ORNAMENT WAS MADE OF COPPER WITH A CHEMICALLY APPLIED PATINA. SUBSEQUENT RELEASES ARE MADE OF 24K GOLD-FINISHED BRASS.

2   *Dove of Peace*

The 1982 White House Christmas Ornament honors President George Washington. Like the design of the first Christmas Ornament, the second is derived from a weather vane, but this one has a specific presidential association. It is modeled on the Dove of Peace weather vane that George Washington commissioned for the cupola atop his Mount Vernon home. The year 1982 also marked the 250th anniversary of George Washington's birth, making the ornament based on his own design a fitting tribute to the first president.

The Dove of Peace recalls the dove Noah sent out from the Ark that returned with an olive branch clasped in its beak. Signaling that the waters of the Great Flood had receded, and that the earth was once again supporting life and bearing fruit, the dove with an olive branch has ever after been a symbol of peace.

In 1787, during the Constitutional Convention in Philadelphia, Washington wrote to a local coppersmith, Joseph Rakestraw: "I would like to have a bird (in place of the Vain) with an olive branch in its Mouth." In the aftermath of the Revolutionary War, the dove with an olive branch was embraced by the nation as a symbol of peace and hope. By placing this symbol atop his own home, Washington affirmed his confidence in the future of the United States. In 1789, within his home and beneath this Dove of Peace, the hero of the American Revolution formally answered the call to become the nation's first president. George Washington never lived in the White House, but he selected its architect, oversaw its design, and last viewed it in the spring of 1797, on his way home, after the presidency, to Mount Vernon.

MEASURING 3 x 3¾ INCHES, THE ORIGINAL ORNAMENT WAS MADE OF COPPER WITH A CHEMICALLY APPLIED PATINA. SUBSEQUENT RELEASES OF THE ORNAMENT ARE MADE OF 24K GOLD-FINISHED BRASS.

President John Adams, 1797–1801

3   *The North Front of the White House*

The 1983 White House Christmas Ornament honors President John Adams with an image of the North Front of the White House as it looked when he lived there. The image is from one of the earliest-known illustrations of the building, an engraving in Charles William Janson's book, *The Stranger in America*, published in London in 1807. Instead of the familiar portico, which would not be built for another thirty years, there was a pediment supported by four Ionic columns attached to the wall of the house. But the swagged garland of richly carved Double Scottish Roses above the door was in place, as it remains today.

President Adams of Massachusetts was the first president to live in the White House. It was not quite finished when he arrived in November 1800. He lighted his rooms with candles and kept warm before large log-burning fireplaces. The house was drafty and uncomfortable, but for Adams it held promise. The next day he wrote his famous benediction for the house in a letter to his wife: "I pray Heaven to bestow the best of Blessings on this House and all that shall hereafter inhabit it. May none but honest and wise Men ever rule under this roof." In 1945 President Franklin D. Roosevelt had the benediction engraved in the stone fireplace mantel in the State Dining Room.

Adams lived in the White House for only four months. His wife Abigail had just joined him when they learned that he had lost his bid for reelection. She called the house "this great castle," "grand and on a superb scale," but so inconvenient that, surrounded by forests, wood for the fireplaces was not to be had. There was as yet no yard, so she hung her laundry to dry in "the great unfinished audience-room" (today's East Room). Nevertheless, on New Year's Day, 1801, she and John Adams welcomed visitors to the White House's first public reception.

MEASURING 2¼ x 2¾ INCHES, THIS ORNAMENT IS MADE OF 24K GOLD-FINISHED BRASS.

President Thomas Jefferson, 1801–1809

4   *Jefferson Peace Medal*

The 1984 White House Christmas Ornament honors President Thomas Jefferson with an image of the historic Jefferson peace medal, minted in 1801. One side of the rotating disk shows the clasped hands of an Indian and a soldier, crowned by a tomahawk and a pipe of peace and inscribed "Peace and Friendship." The other side displays Jefferson's profile with an inscription: "Th. Jefferson President of the U.S. A.D. 1801."

Jefferson was just 33 years old when he wrote the Declaration of Independence. During the Revolution he served as governor of Virginia and in 1785 was sent to Paris as the new nation's minister to France. Returning in 1789, he learned that President George Washington had appointed him secretary of state. He served as vice president to John Adams, and his election as president in 1800 was termed a "Revolution," for putting the Democratic-Republicans in power. As president, Jefferson oversaw the acquisition in 1803 of Louisiana from France, a vast interior territory beyond the Mississippi River that doubled the size of the country. To explore and map the new lands, President Jefferson sent Meriwether Lewis and William Clark on a two-year expedition. When they returned, he displayed the plant and animal specimens they had collected at the White House for the public to enjoy.

Before Lewis and Clark began their journey, Jefferson sent the expedition a supply of peace medals to distribute to the Native American leaders they might meet along the way. In colonial times, the British had given medals to the heads of Indian nations as tokens of friendship, and American presidents continued the practice. By 1801 peace medals had assumed a somewhat standard format, with symbols of peace on one side and a likeness of the president of the United States on the other. Early nineteenth-century Indian portraits by Charles Bird King in the White House collection show that the Indians customarily wore the medals as medallions on ribbons around their necks.

MEASURING 2½ INCHES IN DIAMETER, THE TWO-SIDED ROTATING DISK ORNAMENT IS MADE OF 24K GOLD-FINISHED BRASS.

President James Madison, 1809–1817

5   *Madison Silhouettes*

The 1985 White House Christmas Ornament honors President James Madison with two early silhouettes of the couple famous for the hospitality they brought to the White House. The profile of President Madison, derived from an original by Joseph Sansom, shows the statesman at age 30, a young congressman from Virginia. First Lady Dolley Madison's image is based upon a "hollow-cut silhouette" made by an unknown artist in the late 1780s, when she was a young Philadelphia matron. Their paths had not yet crossed; their greatest achievements and adventures lay before them.

For James Madison of Virginia, the presidency was the peak of a long and distinguished career in public service. He is primarily remembered for his brilliant leadership at the Constitutional Convention of 1787, but he was also Thomas Jefferson's secretary of state. Before that, he served in the First Congress as a representative from Virginia, and it was in Philadelphia, in 1794, that he met and married Dolley Payne Todd. They were a most notable couple, opposite in many ways: James was quiet, intense, and bookish, while Dolley was outgoing and genuinely fond of people. Well into middle age she dressed youthfully, indulging a love of silk turbans. "Everybody likes Mrs. Madison," said Henry Clay, to which she responded, "Mrs. Madison likes everybody."

At the White House the Madisons held weekly receptions that were intended to bring together politicians of opposite views, local citizens, and visitors to the city in a relaxed, social atmosphere. The State Rooms blazed with lamplight, and the fine food and drink was unsurpassed. "Mrs. Madison's Drawing Rooms," as the receptions were called, became the most popular events in the city, and they helped unite Congress behind the president as a second war against Britain loomed. When war came, in 1812, President Madison endured much criticism before a "Christmas peace" was signed at Ghent in 1814. But, the previous August, British troops had burned Washington. First Lady Dolley Madison, remaining at the White House until the last minute, famously made sure that the large portrait of George Washington was removed to safety before she fled.

MEASURING 3¼ INCHES IN DIAMETER, THIS ORNAMENT IS MADE OF 24K GOLD-FINISHED BRASS.

1986
President James Monroe, 1817–1825

6   *The South Portico of the White House*

The 1986 White House Christmas Ornament honors President James Monroe with a depiction of the South Front of the President's House as it appeared in 1824 during Christmas and New Year's festivities.

President James Monroe was the third president from Virginia in a row, and the third to have first served as secretary of state. Monroe also had diplomatic experience, as minister to France and Great Britain. The two terms of his presidency were known then and now as "The Era of Good Feelings," for the patriotism that followed the successful conclusion of the War of 1812 and the decline in partisanship that had preceded it. But the President's House had been burned during that war, and its reconstruction was not quite finished when Monroe's presidency began. He had the enviable task of furnishing it from scratch, and he filled the State Rooms with gilded French furniture and interior decorations carved with representations of the American eagle.

From the White House Monroe signed the doctrine that bears his name, a proclamation that henceforth Americans would stay out of Europe's wars, and Europe should stay out of the Americas. He believed that the nation had come of age, and the White House became his prime symbol. To the South Front he decided to add a portico and called back to work James Hoban, the Irish-born architect and builder originally hired by George Washington to construct the White House. The South Portico was finished entirely in stone. Plain but handsome and massive, it was fitted with wrought-iron railings and supported from beneath by stone vaulting. The columns rise some 30 feet. Completed in 1824, the South Portico is the defining feature of the South Front. It wraps around the bow that contains three levels of famous oval rooms; the best known of these, the Blue Room, opens onto the porch. Though in succeeding years the South Front developed as the private side of the White House, today it also provides a ceremonial backdrop for the arrival of visiting heads of state and other dignitaries.

THIS THREE-DIMENSIONAL ORNAMENT MEASURES 1¾ x 3½ x ¼ INCHES AND IS MADE OF 24K GOLD-FINISHED BRASS WITH ENAMEL COLOR.

1987
President John Quincy Adams, 1825–1829

7 *White House Doors*

The 1987 White House Christmas Ornament honors President John Quincy Adams with a depiction of the sandstone portal and double mahogany doors of the White House, decorated for Christmas with traditional evergreen wreaths. The red poinsettias alongside the doors were first introduced to the United States by Joel Poinsett, Adams's minister to Mexico, who was pleased to thus gratify the president's interest in flowers.

The first son of a president to be president, John Quincy Adams left a lasting mark on the White House gardens. His personal interest in developing and improving the White House Grounds established what is today one of the oldest continually maintained landscapes in the country. During his stormy presidency, his program for gardening was to be his diversion. Like so many predecessors, Adams had diplomatic experience and served as secretary of state. But his election was not clear cut. Of the five candidates running in 1824, none achieved a majority in the Electoral College, so, as the Constitution required, the vote among the top three was put to the House of Representatives. Andrew Jackson had led in electoral and popular votes, but Adams won the runoff, thanks to Henry Clay, who had come in fourth and urged his supporters to vote for Adams. When President Adams then named Clay secretary of state, Jackson's supporters cried "corrupt bargain" and for four years worked to deny Adams a second term. They succeeded.

Although Adams had ambitious plans for internal improvements and a national university and astronomical observatory, his proposals were largely mocked and blocked by Congress. So he found satisfaction in gardening. He met with the White House gardener nearly every day, and together they developed a new flower garden. Adams's special interest in native American trees led to the idea of an arboretum on the White House Grounds. Politicians, tourists, and sea captains often brought him seeds and young trees from their travels. Adams lost to Jackson in 1828, but he was not done with politics. Massachusetts sent him back to Washington as a member of the House of Representatives, where he served for the rest of his life.

THIS THREE-DIMENSIONAL ORNAMENT MEASURES 4 x 2½ x ¼ INCHES AND IS MADE OF 24K GOLD-FINISHED BRASS WITH ENAMEL COLORS.

1988
President Andrew Jackson, 1829–1837

8   *The Children*

The 1988 White House Christmas Ornament honors President Andrew Jackson with an ornament representing a remarkable Christmas Day celebration in 1836 when a party was held for the children of Jackson's family and their friends. There were games and then a march down the long hallway to the State Dining Room, where an elaborate table of cakes, ice cream, and candy awaited the guests. After dinner the children were taken to view a remarkable scene, a pyramid composed of cotton "snowballs." They were invited to step forward, take cotton balls, and have a free-for-all "snowfight." At the end of the evening, the children lined up to bow or curtsy as they said "Good night, General," one by one. The ornament pictures two children admiring a "cotton ball" Christmas tree topped with a rooster and decorated with red ribbon bows. Underneath is the text of the party invitation: "The Children of President Jackson's family request you to join them on Christmas Day at four o'clock P.M., in a frolic in the East Room."

General Andrew Jackson came to the presidency in a landslide and already a legend. He was the hero of the Battle of New Orleans, but he had also served as a congressman and senator from Tennessee and as the military governor of Florida. He was hailed as the representative of the common man, whose interests he would champion during his tenure in the White House. In office, he broke the power of the Second Bank of the United States and stood up against those who threatened to divide the Union over sectional issues.

President Jackson's household was large and his White House was crowded. It included his adopted son and many of his wife's nephews and nieces, together with their numerous little children. In private the Jackson circle lived like country folk, eating plain food and spending their leisure hours together in the upstairs oval room. Downstairs, Jackson finished the East Room, furnishing it on a grand scale for the scores of levees and celebrations he held there.

THIS THREE-DIMENSIONAL ORNAMENT MEASURES 3¼ x 3 x ¼ INCHES AND IS MADE OF 24K GOLD-FINISHED BRASS WITH ENAMEL COLORS.

Christmas 1988   The White House

The Children of President Jackson's family request you to join them on Christmas Day at four o'clock P.M., in a frolic in the East Room

9   *The Presidential Seal*

The 1989 White House Christmas Ornament celebrates the 200th anniversary of the presidency of the United States with a depiction of the Presidential Seal. Around the perimeter is inscribed: "In Celebration of the Bicentennial of the American Presidency."

The first president, General George Washington, hero of the American War for Independence, was at his home, Mount Vernon, in Virginia, on April 14, 1789, when he was informed he had been elected as the first president of the United States. Two days later he departed for the capital in New York, having little idea of what to expect. The office of the president was an American invention, and the very concept of a modern republic, as defined in the Constitution, was entirely new. Washington began his administration with firmness and vision, realizing that anything he did might establish a precedent for the future. Symbols were few for President Washington, beyond the flag. The revolution against a government ruled by a king was so recent as to make people suspicious of such aristocratic decorations as coats of arms.

So even though Congress adopted the Great Seal of the United States in 1782, there was no official Presidential Seal before 1945. There had been earlier versions, all, like the Great Seal, showing an eagle with a banner in its beak proclaiming "E Pluribus Unum," a cluster of arrows in its left talons, and an olive branch in its right talons. In 1850 President Millard Fillmore sketched such a seal and had it engraved, and in 1880 President Rutherford B. Hayes used a version of the seal on White House invitations. Then in 1945 President Harry S. Truman changed the eagle to face the olive branch of peace, not the arrows of war, and made the design official by executive order. Above the eagle's head are thirteen stars and thirteen puffs of clouds, for the thirteen colonies, and around the perimeter are more stars, one for each state. Today there are fifty, the last two added in 1959 by President Dwight D. Eisenhower, for Alaska and Hawaii.

THIS THREE-DIMENSIONAL ORNAMENT MEASURES 3¼ x 3¼ x ¼ INCHES AND IS MADE OF 24K GOLD-FINISHED BRASS WITH ENAMEL COLORS.

In Celebration of the Bicentennial of the American Presidency

1789 THE WHITE HOUSE 1989

1990
President Martin Van Buren, 1837–1841

10 *The Blue Room*

The 1990 White House Christmas Ornament honors President Martin Van Buren with a representation of the Blue Room he established. Since there are no photographs of the room from this time, the White House Historical Association created the view depicted based on the household inventory made when Van Buren left office and the invoices submitted by Washington upholsterer Charles Alexandre. Striped wallpaper and swagged draperies were typical of the time. The chandelier is designed after one in the house during Van Buren's presidency. The two chairs are part of the famous suite of gilded furniture—originally upholstered in crimson—that President James Monroe had ordered from France nineteen years before. Several chairs have since been returned to the White House and, upholstered in blue, are again in the Blue Room today.

The decor of the oval parlor on the State Floor of the White House was changed from red to blue by direction of President Van Buren. When Congress authorized $20,000 for repairs to the President's House, Van Buren summoned Alexandre to redecorate the State Parlors. Alexandre brought his swatches and samples to the president, and Van Buren chose blue for the oval parlor. All the decorations were blue—satin upholstery and curtains, wallpaper, and carpeting. The oval parlor has been decorated in blue, and called the Blue Room, ever since.

Van Buren of New York had been President Andrew Jackson's secretary of state, vice president, and choice as successor. His administration began with high prospects but was soon struck with a national depression. Yet Van Buren, a widower, oversaw a boldly elegant social life in the White House encouraged by his four sons and daughter-in-law and hostess, Angelica Singleton. They planned lively entertainments, with rounds of dinners and dances. Before long, the social activities attracted criticism as an example of official excess during hard times. Van Buren, though a shrewd politician, lost his bid for reelection.

THIS THREE-DIMENSIONAL ORNAMENT MEASURES 3¼ x 3½ x ¼ INCHES AND IS MADE OF 24K GOLD-FINISHED BRASS WITH ENAMEL COLORS.

II   *A White Charger*

The 1991 White House Christmas Ornament honors President William Henry Harrison with a portrayal of him as a general in full military dress astride his white charger, inspired by a painting by Alonzo Pease. A personal friend of Harrison, Platt Rogers Spencer, developed the style of script that is used for the inscription on the ornament: "Christmas 1991 / The White House."

General Harrison of Ohio, the hero of the Battle of Tippecanoe, was elected president in 1840. On March 4, 1841—Inauguration Day—beneath thunderous skies and pouring rain, he wore full military dress and mounted a beautiful white charger for a two-hour procession to the Capitol. There, after taking the Oath of Office, he delivered the longest inaugural address in American history. When that ceremony was finished, the president, again astride his charger, joined a long parade to the White House that included military marchers, bands, and a float portraying a log cabin—Harrison's campaign symbol notwithstanding that he had been born in a grand manor house on a Virginia plantation. Three weeks later Harrison summoned the White House doctor. He felt ill, and soon pneumonia set in. On April 4, he died. He was the first president to die in office and the one who has served the shortest time in the history of the presidency.

Not his presidency but his legacy as a military hero of the Old Northwest firmly places Harrison in American history. He had fought with General Anthony Wayne at the Battle of Fallen Timbers in 1794 and served as governor of the Indiana Territory. In the War of 1812 he defeated the British and their Indian allies at the Battle of the Thames. But Harrison is best remembered for his 1811 battle against an Indian confederation at Tippecanoe Creek in Indiana. Westerners claimed a great victory, and it was as the hero of Tippecanoe that Harrison rose to the presidency.

THIS ORNAMENT MEASURES 3¾ x 3½ INCHES AND IS MADE OF 24K GOLD-FINISHED BRASS WITH ENAMEL COLORS.

12 *200th Anniversary of the Laying of the White House Cornerstone*

The 1992 White House Christmas Ornament marks the 200th anniversary of the laying of the White House cornerstone, which is still somewhere in its walls today. One side of the ornament features a reproduction of an 1848 color lithograph of the North Front of the White House, after a watercolor by Augustus Kollner. This lithograph is one of the best early views of the building. On the other side is the text of the cornerstone as published in the press at the time it was laid: "This first stone of the President's House was laid the 13th day of October 1792 and in the seventeenth year of the independence of the United States of America. . . . Vivat Republica."

President George Washington took a strong interest in planning the President's House. He personally selected the site and the architect, James Hoban, and when construction was about to begin he located the house itself by driving the first stakes into the ground. The Scottish stonemason Collen Williamson began building the stone walls using sandstone from the Aquia Creek quarry on the Potomac River, south of Mount Vernon. According to ancient custom, during construction, when a corner was completed, a cornerstone was set with ceremony to honor the project, bring it luck, and record it for all time. Common in Europe, cornerstones were not usual in America on private houses, but they were common on public buildings, and the White House was a public building as well as a house.

A brief ceremony on October 13, 1792, marked the occasion. In truth the cornerstone was not a stone but a brass plate engraved with the names of the government officials and builders involved, the date, and the inscription, "Vivat Republica," Long Live the Republic. The plate was pressed into a recess in one of the stones, mortar was placed over it, and another stone placed on top. That accomplished, the participants marched to nearby Georgetown to Suter's Fountain Inn, where they celebrated with many toasts. The exact location of the cornerstone was soon forgotten.

THIS TWO-SIDED, THREE DIMENSIONAL ORNAMENT MEASURES 3 x 3½ x ¼ INCHES AND FEATURES A CERAMIC OVAL PRINTED IN COLOR SURROUNDED BY A 24K GOLD-FINISHED BRASS FRAME.

13 *Portrait of First Lady Julia Gardiner Tyler*

The 1993 White House Christmas Ornament honors President John Tyler with a depiction of First Lady Julia Gardiner Tyler's large portrait by Francesco Anelli reduced to resemble a miniature portrait like those given at the time as gifts to special friends and loved ones. After the Civil War, Julia, by then a widow, presented the original oil painting as a gift to the White House. It depicts a younger Julia in voluminous white silk, smiling wistfully beneath a headband of pearls and holding a folded fan. The painting was the first in what is today a comprehensive collection at the White House of portraits of first ladies.

When Julia Gardiner, age 24, wed John Tyler, 54 years old and the president of the United States, the administration's political woes were forgotten for a White House love story. Vice President Tyler of Virginia had become president upon the death of President William Henry Harrison, the first vice president to assume the presidency this way, and the entire cabinet but one had resigned. The next year Tyler's wife, Letitia, died. Soon Tyler began to notice Julia Gardiner, an acclaimed beauty who visited the Tyler children and attended White House social events. His courtship was kept very quiet until a tragedy threw them together. On February 28, 1844, during a Potomac River excursion aboard the navy's new steam frigate *Princeton*, a cannon misfired and exploded. Eight bystanders were killed, including Senator David Gardiner, Julia's father. Four months later, President Tyler and Julia Gardiner were married.

Following a wedding trip, Julia Tyler began a series of parties at the White House that did not stop until her husband's term ended. The table in the State Dining Room was extended to seat forty for long, candlelight dinners, while the East Room was given over to dancing. There with the president's approval, Julia Tyler introduced the waltz to Washington, shocking society.

THIS THREE DIMENSIONAL ORNAMENT MEASURES 3½ x 2¾ x ¼ INCHES AND FEATURES A CERAMIC OVAL PRINTED IN COLOR SURROUNDED BY TWO 24K GOLD-FINISHED BRASS FRAMES WITH ENAMEL COLORS.

President James K. Polk, 1845–1849

14 *The United States Marine Band on the South Lawn of the White House*

The 1994 White House Christmas Ornament honors President James K. Polk with a cameo-style depiction of him and his wife Sarah as they are serenaded by the Marine Band during a public concert on the South Lawn of the White House. Francesco Scala, the leader of the band, stands in front with his drum major's mace in hand. Among the instruments are trombones, a clarinet, and the long ophicleide that was the predecessor of the tuba. The scene is imaginary but meticulously researched, the blue and red uniforms of the Marine Band are accurate in every detail. The depiction of the South Front of the President's House is based on John Plumbe's daguerreotype taken in the winter of 1846. Photography had been invented only seven years earlier.

The United States Marine Band, which President James K. Polk described in his diary as "the Band of Music," was by his time a White House institution. Established in 1798, when the capital was still in Philadelphia, the Marine Band was introduced to the White House by President John Adams on New Year's Day in 1801, and it was nicknamed "The President's Own" by Thomas Jefferson. For President Polk, the Marine Band provided music for lawn concerts, dinners, and receptions, but not for dancing, which First Lady Sarah Polk prohibited in the White House, along with whiskey punches. She did, however, initiate the custom of having the band announce the president's entrance with "Hail to the Chief."

Polk was, in fact, a most notable commander in chief. A Tennessee protégé of Andrew Jackson, he had run for president on an expansionist platform, and he carried out his promises. Texas was officially annexed right after his first Christmas in office. Settling a boundary dispute with Great Britain, he incorporated Oregon Territory. And the war with Mexico brought vast new lands in the Southwest into the Union. As his last Christmas in office approached, President Polk revealed that gold had been discovered in California, so recently won from Mexico. By Christmas the Gold Rush was on.

THIS THREE-DIMENSIONAL ORNAMENT IS 3 x 3½ x ¼ INCHES AND FEATURES A CERAMIC CAMEO PRINTED IN COLOR SURROUNDED BY A 24K GOLD-FINISHED BRASS FRAME WITH ENAMEL COLORS.

President Zachary Taylor, 1849–1850

15 *A Patriotic Christmas*

The 1995 White House Christmas Ornament honors President Zachary Taylor, with a patriotic view of the White House draped in flags, each with thirty stars for the number of states in the Union at the time of Taylor's election. Between the flags is an eagle with trumpets, arrows, and more flags—a motif inspired by a Zachary Taylor paper window shade made about the time of his inauguration.

General Zachary Taylor was the fourth military hero to serve as president and the second to die in office. His leadership during the Mexican War won him the 1848 presidential election and a place in national memory as "Old Rough and Ready," the affectionate nickname given to him by his soldiers. He had a long career in the army, serving in campaigns against Native American resistance in the West and in Florida. In 1845 he was commander of the First Department of the Western Division of the Army when President James K. Polk ordered him to Texas. The next year Polk ordered him to the Rio Grande, across a border-land claimed by both the United States and Mexico. The action initiated war, and for months General Taylor's exploits were front-page news. At Buena Vista, he won a great victory. The war over, Taylor returned to Louisiana and was at home in Baton Rouge when he learned he had been nominated for president.

President Taylor's large family moved into the White House. At social functions, one of his daughters generally presided. On July 4, 1850, he attended patriotic ceremonies on the grounds of the unfinished Washington Monument. It was hot, and he drank ice water liberally, then ate a prodigious number of chilled fresh cherries that the White House cook placed before him. By nightfall he felt ill. Pale and trembling, he began to fail before the eyes of those who stood watch around his bed. Sinking into delirium, Taylor died on July 9. The doctors diagnosed acute cholera.

MEASURING 3¼ x 3 x ¼ INCHES, THIS THREE-DIMENSIONAL ORNAMENT FEATURES A WHITE BISQUE PORCELAIN SCULPTURAL RELIEF AND 24K GOLD-FINISHED BRASS WITH ENAMEL COLORS.

The White House
Christmas 1995

1996
President Millard Fillmore, 1850–1853

16 *The First Presidential Seal*

The 1996 White House Christmas Ornament honors President Millard Fillmore with a depiction of the Presidential Seal of his design. The seal adopts the bald eagle with arrows in one talon, for war, and an olive branch in the other, for peace. Surrounding the eagle are thirty-one stars, one for each state of the Union in 1850, the year Fillmore became president. On the ornament, the seal is set against a backdrop of the North Portico of the White House in 1850, looking exactly the same today, from Pennsylvania Avenue, as it did then.

As vice president, Millard Fillmore remained a relatively obscure New York politician until the unexpected death of President Zachary Taylor made him president. Though still not notable among presidents, Fillmore had accomplishments, Primarily his promoting and then signing of Congress's Compromise of 1850, which stilled sectional tensions, at least for a while. Pursuing overseas trade, Fillmore encouraged Commodore Matthew C. Perry's expedition to Japan. He also initiated the plan for the completion of the U.S. Capitol, with wings and a giant dome. Inside the White House, First Lady Abigail Fillmore, formerly a teacher, installed a library in the upstairs oval room, with custom-made bookcases that ringed the curving walls.

Not three weeks after taking office, Fillmore sketched out his idea for a new Presidential Seal that would be impressed into hot wax as a means of embellishing and endorsing official presidential papers. Fillmore sent his sketch to Edward Stabler in Sandy Spring, Maryland, a seal-maker and engraver of fine reputation. Stabler engraved an improved version of Fillmore's design on a "hard composition of metal known as bell metal." The president approved, and Stabler began producing the seals at $20 each for presidential and White House use.

MEASURING 3 INCHES IN DIAMETER AND ¼ INCH IN DEPTH, THIS THREE-DIMENSIONAL ORNAMENT IS MADE OF 24K GOLD-FINISHED BRASS WITH ENAMEL COLORS.

1997
President Franklin Pierce, 1853–1857

17 *White House Renovations*

The 1997 White House Christmas Ornament honors President Franklin Pierce by commemorating his White House renovations made in 1853 and 1854. The highly ornamented frame, based on the frames of two elaborate mirrors Pierce hung in the State Rooms, suggests the rich character of the Pierce's White House furnishings. In the center, on a ceramic tablet, is a tranquil view from 1857 that depicts the White House with visitors strolling on the South Lawn. The private greenhouse President Pierce constructed can be seen on the west.

Franklin Pierce of New Hampshire remained a popular president even as sectional tensions increased during the 1850s. His administration was notable for promoting a transcontinental railroad and the addition of the Gadsden Purchase, which provided a potential southern right-of-way for a rail line. Privately, he and his wife, First Lady Jane Appleton Pierce, never stopped mourning the death of their only surviving son, just two months before his inauguration.

The Pierces oversaw a renovation of the White House that was the most extensive since the time of James Monroe. Furniture, carpeting, mirrors, gas chandeliers, marble lavatories in the bedrooms spouting cold Potomac water, steam heating, a kitchen range, and an icebox transformed the White House into a handsome and convenient modern setting for presidential entertaining. On the White House Grounds, Pierce's greenhouse with a glass ceiling was added to Andrew Jackson's tall-windowed orangery and styled as a sitting room with cast-iron furnishings. The greenhouse gave the Pierces a place to enjoy plants and flowers in a space set apart from the lawns of the White House, which were open to the public several days a week. When the planned completion of the Treasury Building on the east meant that the greenhouse would have to be demolished, Pierce had another greenhouse built on the west, connected to the White House, so his successors would not be deprived of the private retreat.

THIS THREE-DIMENSIONAL ORNAMENT MEASURES 3¼ x 3¼ x ¼ INCHES AND FEATURES A CERAMIC TABLET PRINTED IN COLOR, SURROUNDED BY A 24K GOLD-FINISHED BRASS FRAME.

Christmas 1997

1998
President James Buchanan, 1857–1861

18 *The American Bald Eagle and Shield*

The 1998 White House Christmas Ornament honors President James Buchanan with a design that recalls the time of his "republican court" and it borrows from the romantic garlands and wreaths with which his niece and hostess Harriet Lane decorated the White House. The ornament depicts the eagle and shield insignia that appeared on the glassware used by President Buchanan. Surrounding the eagle is a wreath of white blossoms from the famous Jackson Magnolia from the White House South Lawn and of red camellias that Harriet Lane grew in the greenhouse attached to the White House. An inscription carries the traditional U.S. motto "E Pluribus Unum," Out of Many, One.

James Buchanan of Pennsylvania—militiaman, congressman, overseas diplomat, senator, and secretary of state—seemed well qualified to lead the nation in the dangerous time ahead of the Civil War. Socially, he was ably assisted by Harriet Lane. She redecorated some of the State Rooms, purchasing new, heavily carved French-style pieces finished in gold leaf and setting out vases of fresh-cut flowers in the English fashion. Her frequent receptions and elegant entertaining led some to compare Buchanan's White House to a royal, or "republican" court. Yet the social pace and the splendid entertainments—for Britain's Prince of Wales, for example, and for the first delegation, ever, from Japan—so enjoyed at the time, were actually a veneer over political hostility that only grew more tense. This was the last time all the political luminaries of the 1850s would gather in the White House before the war split them apart.

THIS THREE-DIMENSIONAL ORNAMENT MEASURES 3 x 2¾ x ¼ INCHES AND FEATURES A WHITE BISQUE PORCELAIN EAGLE SURROUNDED BY A 24K GOLD-FINISHED BRASS FRAME WITH ENAMEL COLORS.

1999
President Abraham Lincoln, 1861-1865

19   *Portrait of President Abraham Lincoln*

The 1999 White House Christmas Ornament honors President Abraham Lincoln with a depiction of his portrait by George P. A. Healy displayed in a hinged frame adapted from a Civil War era ambrotype or tintype frame in the White House collection. The frame opens like a locket. The interior frame bears the inscription: "The union now and forever." On the reverse is a facsimile of Lincoln's signature.

No president has left a more enduring mark on the White House than Abraham Lincoln. He rose from humble origins in the log cabin woods of Kentucky to practice law in Illinois and then to guide his country through its greatest crisis, the Civil War. Under his leadership slavery was ended and the broken Union mended. His tenure in the White House covered just a month over four years, but his legacy is timeless. The tragedy of his life there, and that of his family, symbolized so compellingly the tragedies of many families north and south during the war that the White House was in a sense sanctified by it. Every president to follow would seek to understand Lincoln in the many facets of his presidency, but also, and profoundly, to contemplate the personal sacrifice greatness exacted from the man.

In 1864, the leading portrait artist George P. A. Healy began a painting of President Lincoln, but, with the end of the Civil War imminent, soon turned to a group portrait of the president, General Ulysses S. Grant, General William T. Sherman, and Rear Admiral David D. Porter to commemorate the men who ended the conflict. With *The Peacemakers* completed in 1868, Congress commissioned Healy to paint a portrait of the late President Lincoln for the White House. For his painting, completed in 1869, Healy adapted the figure of Lincoln from the group portrait. This Lincoln portrait now hangs over the fireplace in the State Dining Room.

MEASURING 3 x 2½ x ½ INCHES THIS HINGED THREE DIMENSIONAL ORNAMENT FEATURES A CERAMIC OVAL PRINTED IN COLOR SURROUNDED BY TWO 24K GOLD-FINISHED BRASS FRAMES.

200th Anniversary of the White House

20 *The North and South Fronts of the White House*

The White House Christmas Ornament for the year 2000 commemorates the 200th anniversary of the White House with two highly detailed white sculptural reliefs of the mansion's North and South Fronts on a rotating center stone. The stone is made of sandstone from the very quarry in Aquia, Virginia, that produced the sandstone for the original exterior walls of the White House. These sculptural reliefs were created in a mold by mixing the sandstone, crushed to a fine powder, with resin.

On November 1, 1800, President John Adams moved into the not-quite-finished White House, but he was required to do so by law, for the Residence Act of 1790 mandated that, "prior to the first Monday in December, in the year one thousand eight hundred," all government offices be removed to the new Federal District on the Potomac River. Adams spent a long afternoon greeting well-wishers, ate supper by himself, and in the evening climbed the twisting service stairs to his bedchamber to sleep. The next day, in a letter to his wife Abigail, he penned his now famous prayer: "I pray Heaven to bestow the best of Blessings on this House and all that shall hereafter inhabit it. May none but honest and wise Men ever rule under this roof." In 1945 President Franklin D. Roosevelt ordered Adams's benediction carved on the stone fireplace mantel in the State Dining Room, where it can be seen today.

Since the night Adams penned his prayer, the White House has endured to be the oldest continually occupied official residence of a head of state in the world. In 2000, the White House Historical Association marked the 200th anniversary of the home of the president with a celebration at the White House hosted by President Bill Clinton and First Lady Hillary Clinton and attended by President and Mrs. Gerald Ford, President and Mrs. Jimmy Carter, President and Mrs. George H. W. Bush, and Former First Lady Lady Bird Johnson. The presidents toasted the great history of the White House, and each spoke of how he had been influenced by the White House. The Association also donated a new State China Service featuring architectural and decorative elements from the White House. Celebrations included a reenactment of John Adams arriving at the back door of the White House in a horse-drawn carriage.

MEASURING 3¼ x 3¾ x ½ INCHES, THIS THREE-DIMENSIONAL ORNAMENT FEATURES A CENTRAL TWO-SIDED ROTATING OVAL OF AQUIA SANDSTONE EMBEDDED IN RESIN SURROUNDED BY A 24K GOLD-FINISHED BRASS FRAME WITH ENAMEL COLORS.

The
WHITE HOUSE

200TH ANNIVERSARY
CHRISTMAS 2000

President Andrew Johnson, 1865–1869

21   *A First Family's Carriage Ride*

The 2001 White House Christmas Ornament honors President Andrew Johnson by capturing the joyous spirit of a family outing in a nostalgic winter scene. The three-dimensional carriage ornament depicts the president with his children and grandchildren, returning to the White House from an afternoon carriage ride at Christmastime. An 1867 photograph of the South Front of the White House inspired the engraved-style illustration.

Andrew Johnson of Tennessee, a pro-Union southerner and Democrat, was added to President Abraham Lincoln's reelection ticket in 1864 in the hopes of attracting votes from "War Democrats." When, after Lincoln's assassination, Johnson rose to the presidency, he found himself isolated and much despised by the radical Republicans in Congress, who challenged his conservative plans for reconstructing the Union following the Civil War. Johnson was the first president to be impeached, though he was not removed from office by trial in the Senate. The administration did have significant accomplishments, however, especially the ratification of the Thirteenth Amendment, ending slavery, and the Fourteenth Amendment, establishing citizenship and civil rights for former slaves. The purchase of Alaska from Russia, though mocked at the time, was another lasting legacy of the era.

When Johnson moved into the White House, he brought with him his grown children and their families, so altogether five grandchildren. With the political turmoil surrounding his presidency, Johnson's life at the White House might have been unbearable had it not been for the love of this close-knit family. The president relaxed most when he was with his children and grandchildren. He often took afternoon carriage rides with them through the rolling farm roads that crossed the forest, meadows, and fields of what twenty years later would become Rock Creek Park. Occasionally the family would picnic along the picturesque creek in the grassy meadows near Pierce Mill. Just after Christmas in 1868, the president held a White House party for his grandchildren, with much dancing in the East Room.

MEASURING 2¼ X 4½ X ½ INCHES, THIS THREE-DIMENSIONAL ORNAMENT IS MADE OF 24K GOLD-FINISHED BRASS WITH ENAMEL COLORS.

22 *The South Front of the White House*

The 2002 White House Christmas Ornament celebrates the centennial of President Theodore Roosevelt's renovation of the White House with an engraving of the South Front on a central clear disk that recalls the sparkling Bohemian glass of the elegant East Room chandeliers. The decorative frame includes a holiday ribbon, acanthus leaves from the East Room's Louis XVI-style wall panels, and a sturdy eagle, inspired by the carved mahogany pedestals of the new console tables designed for the East Room.

The White House was 102 years old when President Theodore Roosevelt began his major renovation in 1902. Under the direction of New York architects, McKim, Mead & White, it was completely transformed to become the home and office of the president that we recognize today. The architects used the original eighteenth-century design of the house as a springboard and then overhauled the interiors and functional layout. By removing the stair hall, they enlarged the State Dining Room and paneled its walls in waxed oak. They also paneled the walls of the East Room in the French manner and painted them white. The three State Rooms—the Red Room, the Blue Room, and the Green Room—were give new ribbed silk or velvet wall coverings and furnished with reproductions of French and English antiques.

The entire Second Floor was then given over to family quarters as—most significantly—the president's offices were moved into a separate building on the west grounds that evolved into the West Wing. On the east side of the house, a new social entrance was constructed on foundations for a wing that had been first built by President Thomas Jefferson. The architects pared back the exterior of the White House to the original Palladian architectural design by removing the nineteenth-century greenhouses: they were in the way of the president's new office in any case. The restoration began on June 20, 1902, and was completed in just five months.

MEASURING 3½ x 3¾ x ¼ INCHES, THIS THREE-DIMENSIONAL ORNAMENT FEATURES A CRYSTAL-LIKE ACRYLIC CORE WITH AN ETCHED IMAGE SURROUNDED BY A 24K GOLD-FINISHED BRASS FRAME WITH ENAMEL COLORS.

2003
President Ulysses S. Grant, 1869–1877

23 *A Child's Rocking Horse*

The 2003 White House Christmas Ornament commemorates President Ulysses S. Grant's generous spirit and engaging family with a depiction of a boy on the rocking horse inspired by a Victorian illustration of a child's joy at Christmas. The rocking horse actually rocks, swinging with it a toy train below, its steam locomotive a symbol of the industrial age. Toys of the type available at Washington's fancy goods stores during the Grant administration adorn the encircling wreath.

President Ulysses S. Grant and his family in the White House offered a stable image of peace, domestic affection, and the good life to a nation shaken by war, assassination, and a presidential impeachment trial. The beloved Civil War hero and his wife, First Lady Julia Grant, were doting parents of three boys and one girl. The Grants were known to give generously to charities in Washington, D.C., and during Christmastime, they sent elaborate gift barrels of confections and fruit to institutions caring for the orphans of families torn apart by the Civil War. Mrs. Grant eagerly purchased Christmas presents for relatives and friends and often led groups of children to local shops and bought them toys and candy.

Although he had graduated from the U.S. Military Academy at West Point and fought with distinction during the Mexican War, Grant was working as a clerk in the family's leather goods store in Galena, Illinois, when the Civil War began. He rejoined the U.S. Army as a volunteer, was soon a colonel, then a brigadier general, and after the Battle of Shiloh, a two-star general. Capturing Vicksburg on the Mississippi River, he was the next year commissioned a three-star general, the first to hold the rank since George Washington. His terms for the Confederate surrender at Appomattox Court House in Virginia were a model of humanity and reconciliation. Grant's leadership and popularity made his involvement in politics and his election as president inevitable.

MEASURING 3½ x 3¾ x ½ INCHES, THIS THREE-DIMENSIONAL HAND-PAINTED ORNAMENT FEATURES A COLD-CAST PORCELAIN FIGURE ATTACHED WITH A SWINGING MECHANISM TO A 24K GOLD-FINISHED BRASS WREATH WITH ENAMEL COLORS.

2004
President Rutherford B. Hayes, 1877–1881

24 *A First Family's Sleigh Ride*

The 2004 White House Christmas Ornament honors President Rutherford B. Hayes with a three-dimensional vignette of his family taking a snowy sleigh ride on the North Lawn of the White House. Behind the horse-drawn sleigh is an image of the North Front. The reverse of the ornament shimmers with white snowflakes against an enameled royal blue sky and the inscription: "A winter sleigh ride with President and Mrs. Hayes, 1880."

Rutherford B. Hayes of Ohio came to office after one of the most controversial elections in American history. With wild threats of violence circulating, he took the Oath of Office in private, in the Red Room of the White House, a day before the public ceremony at the Capitol. Determined to set a moral example that countered the excesses of the Gilded Age, he and his wife, First Lady Lucy Webb Hayes, eliminated alcohol and wine from presidential entertainments. A pragmatic reformer, President Hayes served with integrity and honor. He installed the first telephone and the first typewriter in the White House, and with his wife initiated the first significant art collecting at the White House by acquiring portraits of the presidents and especially of first ladies.

With their five children, the Hayeses were an active household at the White House, enjoying such family-centered events Sunday evening hymn sings. At Easter, they invited the children of Washington, D.C., to roll their Easter eggs on the White House Lawn, beginning a tradition that remains a popular public event to this day. Christmases were celebrated with family cheer and merrymaking. Mrs. Hayes ensured that each member of the White House staff received a personal card and a present. President Hayes loved the holiday season and said that wintry weather invigorated him. He enjoyed taking his family and guests out on sleigh rides in the hills around Washington, with sleigh bells jingling.

MEASURING 3½ x 3 x ½ INCHES, THIS TWO-SIDED, THREE-DIMENSIONAL ORNAMENT IS MADE OF 24K GOLD-FINISHED BRASS WITH ENAMEL COLORS.

2005
President James A. Garfield, 1881

25 *The South Front of the White House*

The 2005 White House Christmas Ornament honors President James A. Garfield with an illustration of the South Front of the White House inspired by a period engraving. The color scheme and highly decorative wreath design are derived from art objects, including the family china, needlework, and historic frames in the collection at Lawnfield, the historic Garfield house in Mentor, Ohio. The "JAG" monogram on the ornament is styled after that used in Garfield's Inaugural Ball decorations, which now hang at Lawnfield. On the reverse is an etching of the South Front.

President Garfield was a preacher, teacher, military general, lawyer, politician, and the last president born in a log cabin. He had served in the U.S. House of Representatives and was elected to the Senate before also winning the Republican nomination and then the presidency. He and his wife, Lucretia (called "Crete"), brought five young children with them, as well as his mother, when they moved into the White House. They were an affectionate family who enjoyed each other's company, but they spent no Christmases in the White House.

On July 2, 1881, just four months after his inauguration, President Garfield was shot twice by an assassin as he was walking through a Washington railroad station, on the way to join his family at Long Branch, New Jersey, for the summer. Severely wounded, the president was returned to the White House, where in an upstairs bedroom he endured pain, summer heat, and the regular probing by doctors hoping to locate and remove the bullet lodged near his spine. Infection set in. At last, and weakened, he was taken to the New Jersey seaside, in the hopes that the sea air would aid recuperation. He briefly seemed to rally, but, on September 19, he died. Garfield served the second shortest presidential term and was the second president to be assassinated.

MEASURING 3¼ x 3¼ x ½ INCHES, THIS TWO-SIDED, THREE-DIMENSIONAL ORNAMENT FEATURES AN ACRYLIC DOME OVER A COLOR IMAGE SURROUNDED BY A 24K GOLD-FINISHED BRASS WREATH WITH ENAMEL COLORS.

26 *Tiffany Glass in the White House*

The 2006 White House Christmas Ornament honors President Chester A. Arthur with an ornament inspired by the rich decor of his White House. In the center, beneath an American bald eagle, is the North Portico of the White House. Two flanking ovals, translucent like stained glass, depict the stylized American dogwood blossoms that Louis Comfort Tiffany incorporated in a stained glass screen made for the White House Entrance Hall. The leaves on the outer wreath of the ornament are derived from murals painted in the Entrance Hall. The honeysuckle details ("anthemia") in the inner oval frame are adapted from the Victorian decoration of Arthur's East Room. President Arthur's signature is inscribed on the reverse.

Chester A. Arthur was a New York politician associated with political bosses until his unexpected rise to the presidency following President James Garfield's death. He then quickly distanced himself from his roots in New York politics and oversaw the passage of the Pendleton Act, which reformed the Civil Service by curbing the practice of rewarding supporters with federal jobs.

President Arthur loved entertaining and brought to the White House a luxurious style that signaled the nation's prosperity. Most notable was his undertaking a redecoration led by the famed American artist and decorator Louis Comfort Tiffany, known for his use of gold leaf, mosaics, and exotic motifs. Tiffany's most impressive accomplishment in the Arthur White House was the unique opalescent glass screen in the Entrance Hall, a mosaic of shades of ruby, crimson, white, cobalt, and blue that suggested the colors of the American flag. The beautiful glass installation delighted visitors until it was removed in 1902.

MEASURING 3½ x 3 x ½ INCHES THIS THREE-DIMENSIONAL ORNAMENT IS MADE OF 24K GOLD-FINISHED BRASS WITH ENAMEL COLORS.

27   *A President Marries in the White House*

The 2007 White House Christmas Ornament honors the first administration of President Grover Cleveland with a depiction of his 1886 White House wedding to Frances Folsom. The central illustration is a tinted reproduction of an engraving of the bride and groom taking their vows that originally appeared in *Frank Leslie's Illustrated Magazine*. The surrounding frame showcases design elements from the Clevelands' wedding certificate album. On the front, the groom's monogram anchors a decorative border of orange blossoms suggesting Mrs. Cleveland's wedding gown. The back of the ornament features the bride's monogram and reads, "The First Presidential White House Wedding / Grover Cleveland / Frances Folsom / June 2, 1886."

Grover Cleveland was the first Democrat elected president after the Civil War, the only president to serve two nonconsecutive terms, and the only president to marry in the White House. He had been mayor of Buffalo and governor of New York before running for president. He entered the White House as a bachelor, working long hours and rarely entertaining. His sister acted as first lady and managed the affairs of the residence. The public viewed the White House as a quiet, lonely place.

Then on May 28, 1886, the engagement of the president was announced. For more than a year he had secretly courted Frances Folsom, the daughter of his late law partner. As administrator of his partner's estate, Cleveland had devoted himself to the welfare of Folsom's widow and daughter. The courtship came later, and was conducted privately. On June 2, 1886, the 49-year-old president married 21-year-old Frances Folsom in the Blue Room. The bride wore an elegant gown of heavy corded satin draped in frail, pearl white India silk, edged in real orange blossoms, with a 15-foot silk train. Her long silk veil was held in place with orange blossoms and seed pearls.

MEASURING 3 x 3 x ½ INCHES THIS TWO-SIDED, THREE-DIMENSIONAL ORNAMENT IS MADE OF 24K GOLD-FINISHED BRASS WITH TINTED ILLUSTRATION AND ENAMEL COLOR.

President Benjamin Harrison, 1889–1893

28 *A Victorian Christmas Tree*

The 2008 White House Christmas Ornament honors the administration of President Benjamin Harrison with an ornament inspired by the first White House Christmas tree. It is laden with baubles and garlands, projecting the joyous holiday spirit. Beneath the tree are the presents the Harrison grandchildren received that year: a toy train, a wooden sled, building blocks, a rosy-cheeked doll on a tricycle, and a dollhouse. A figure of Santa Claus completes the spectacle. The back of the ornament is inscribed with a quotation from the president: "We shall have an old-fashioned Christmas tree."

President Benjamin Harrison, grandson of President William Henry Harrison, was a centennial president, inaugurated one hundred years after George Washington. He was also the fourth Ohio-born Republican general of the Union Army to serve as president since the Civil War. But it was as an Indianapolis lawyer and senator from Indiana that he gained political prominence. Nominated for president at the 1888 Republican Convention, Harrison conducted one of the first "front porch" campaigns, delivering short speeches to delegations that visited him. The key issue of the election was the tariff, which Harrison pledged to raise if elected, and he did.

Family life was important to Harrison. His daughter's family lived in the White House, and his son's family often visited. The antics of grandchildren on the White House lawn were affectionately reported and photographed in the press. The president was often seen there playing with his grandchildren and their pets, including a goat called His Whiskers. To the delight of the grandchildren, on their first Christmas in the White House, President Harrison placed a Christmas tree in the family library on the Second Floor and had the room decorated with holly, ferns, and sprigs of mistletoe. It was the first time a Christmas tree is known to have been put up in the White House, and on that Christmas morning in 1889 it was surrounded by toys and gifts.

MEASURING 3¾ x 2½ x ¼ INCHES THIS TWO-SIDED, THREE-DIMENSIONAL ORNAMENT IS MADE OF 24K GOLD-FINISHED BRASS WITH ENAMEL COLORS.

WHITE HOUSE CHRISTMAS 2008

President Grover Cleveland, 1893–1897

29 *The First Christmas Tree with Electric Lights*

The 2009 White House Christmas Ornament honors the second administration of President Grover Cleveland with a Christmas scene enjoyed by his young family. The central hologram depicts the South Front of the White House after an evening snowfall in 1894. The warm glow of the first Christmas tree to be illuminated by electric lights is seen through the tall windows of the Second Floor oval room, between the columns. The reverse of the ornament shows a silhouetted scene from the annual tree-trimming parties President and Mrs. Cleveland held for their children and those of cabinet members. It is inscribed with a newspaper account of Christmas in the White House: "There will be a great Christmas tree gorgeous in its beautiful trimmings, 'all sorts and conditions of dolls,' and toys of every description." A finely crafted wreath of snowflakes, painted ice blue and white, frames the oval ornament.

Upon leaving the White House after President Cleveland's first term in 1889, First Lady Frances Folsom Cleveland told staff members that she would be back. And in four years she was. Grover Cleveland was elected to a second term in 1892, the only president to serve two nonconsecutive terms. His family was larger now, and before the end of this second term it would include three daughters. The young children brought life and joy to the White House. More than 20,000 people attended the now annual Easter Monday Egg Roll.

But a panic and an economic depression soon set in, and the rest of Cleveland's second term was marked by turmoil and hardship. In foreign affairs, however, the administration was notable for receiving the first full-rank ambassador to the United States, a sign of the nation's growing international stature. Despite hard times, Cleveland's presidency was personally gratifying to him because of the love of his family. The Christmas holidays naturally focused on the children, and Mrs. Cleveland made the Christmas tree, trimmed in electric lights and laden with toys, the center of the White House holiday decorations.

MEASURING 3 x 3 x ½ INCHES THIS TWO SIDED, THREE-DIMENSIONAL ORNAMENT FEATURES A HOLOGRAPHIC PRINT SURROUNDED BY A 24K GOLD-FINISHED BRASS WREATH WITH ENAMEL COLORS.

President William McKinley, 1897–1901

30   *The Army and Navy Reception at the White House*

The 2010 White House Christmas Ornament honors President William McKinley with festive, colorful scenes from the annual Army and Navy Reception in 1900. The front of the ornament depicts the U.S. Marine Band performing on the snow-covered North Drive as arriving guests disembark from their carriages. The surrounding frame features columns from the East Room, flags, and, at the top, the musical notes for the opening bars of "Hail to the Chief." The reverse of the ornament shows the band playing patriotic airs for the president and his wife Ida, who is dressed in white, in the flag-bedecked splendor of the East Room. The inscriptions read: "The Stars and Stripes Forever / Army Navy Reception 1900."

The American people idolized McKinley. Fatherly and conservative, he endorsed American values, family, and honor. On Sundays the McKinleys invited friends to the White House to sing hymns accompanied by a pianist in the Blue Room. In the East Room, they held "musicales"—short concerts for invited guests. Yet their White House was a quiet place. Years before, they had lost two young daughters, and Ida Saxton McKinley ever after struggled with epilepsy and depression. McKinley was devoted to his wife and protected her.

The William McKinley administration is remembered as a time when the nation moved beyond its continental boundaries to become an international power. In 1898, following victory in the Spanish-American War, the United States gained its first overseas possessions—Guam, Puerto Rico, and the Philippines—and it was at this time, also, that Hawaii was annexed. Like many of his immediate predecessors, McKinley was a Republican Union officer born in Ohio. He had served as a congressman and then governor of Ohio before his election as president. He won a second term, but in 1901 he was murdered by an assassin in Buffalo, New York, where he was attending the Pan-American Exposition. He was the third president to be assassinated in less than forty years.

MEASURING 2¾ x 2 ¾ x ½ INCHES THIS TWO-SIDED THREE DIMENSIONAL ORNAMENT FEATURES A CERAMIC TABLET PRINTED IN COLOR ON TWO SIDES, SURROUNDED BY A 24K GOLD-FINISHED BRASS FRAME WITH A NICKEL COATING AND ENAMEL COLORS.

The Stars and Stripes Forever

Army Navy Reception, 1900

2011
President Theodore Roosevelt, 1901–1909

31 *Santa Visits the White House*

The 2011 White House Christmas Ornament honors President Theodore Roosevelt with illustrations capturing the excitement associated with his family's first White House Christmas. On the front is a color illustration derived from a cartoon by William A. Rogers in 1901, showing Santa Claus crossing the snow-covered North Lawn carrying a bag of toys and announcing, "I hear that there are some kids in the White House this year." The image on the reverse shows the moment when Roosevelt's young son Archie revealed a Christmas tree he had hidden in a seamstress's closet in the White House. The tree defied the president's ban, for he had a strict conservation ethic, and its discovery became a popular Christmas story.

When Vice President Theodore Roosevelt took the Oath of Office in September 1901, following the death of President William McKinley, he was just 42, and the youngest president in the nation's history. He brought vigor and power to the office, initiating progressive reforms at home and recognition abroad. As president, Roosevelt believed that government should be the arbiter between capital and labor, and he earned the nickname "Trustbuster" for regulating large corporations. In foreign policy, he constructed a canal across Panama, shortening the route from the Atlantic to the Pacific. For mediating the treaty ending the Russo-Japanese War, he won the Nobel Peace Prize.

In one of his earliest acts as president, Roosevelt issued an executive order establishing "The White House" as the official name of the presidential residence. The arrival of the Roosevelt family with six children brought new life to the old mansion, and the "strenuous endeavor" that marked all Roosevelt activities was on display. The president romped with his children, and the children, in turn, were famous for antics such as roller skating in the East Room and taking their pony Algonquin upstairs in the elevator. Following a major renovation, the entire Second Floor was now family quarters, and the president had a new office in what would eventually become known as the West Wing.

MEASURING 2½ x 3 x ½ INCHES, THIS TWO-SIDED, THREE-DIMENSIONAL ORNAMENT, FEATURES A CENTRAL TABLET PRINTED IN COLOR ON TWO SIDES, SURROUNDED BY A 24K GOLD-FINISHED BRASS FRAME WITH ENAMEL COLORS.

"I hear there are some kids in the
White House this year."

WHITE HOUSE CHRISTMAS 2011

32 *The First Presidential Automobile*

The 2012 White House Christmas Ornament honors President William Howard Taft with a three-dimensional depiction of the president and his wife Helen en route to deliver Christmas presents in their White Motor Company Model M, a seven-passenger steam-powered touring car embellished with the Great Seal of the United States on the doors. His chauffeur, George H. Robinson, is at the wheel.

President William Howard Taft introduced the automobile to White House transportation in 1909, signifying his ready acceptance of modernity. While secretary of war, he had been smitten with the White steamer, a steam-powered touring car manufactured by the White Sewing Machine Company of Cleveland, Ohio. Taft believed in the future of the automobile, and, as president, he traveled not only in his White steamer but in two Pierce-Arrow limousines. George H. Robinson, Taft's "daredevil" chauffeur, was known for his "fast work at the wheel." But the president, it was reported, "has the real speed fever, and Robinson knows it."

In the White House, the Tafts were a wholesome and busy family. Only one son was still at home and two older children were in college. President Taft doubled the size of the executive office Theodore Roosevelt had built and created the first Oval Office. First Lady Helen Herron Taft took an active role in the planning of Potomac Drive for automobiles and the enhancement of Potomac Park with flowering cherry trees, a gift from Japan, that are still among Washington's loveliest attractions. She had first seen the Japanese cherry trees while her husband was civil governor of the Philippines. The couple had returned from Asia to Washington so Taft could join Roosevelt's cabinet. He had been Roosevelt's choice for president and pledged to continue the progressive Roosevelt agenda. Taft did prosecute antitrust violations, but he broke his promise in supporting higher tariffs and selling public lands in the West. Challenged by Roosevelt, Taft lost reelection. But the Supreme Court, not the presidency, had been Taft's ambition all along, and he achieved it in 1921, when he became chief justice.

MEASURING 2 x 3½ x ¾ INCHES THIS THREE-DIMENSIONAL ORNAMENT IS MADE OF 24K GOLD-FINISHED BRASS WITH A NICKEL COATING AND ENAMEL COLORS.

2013
President Woodrow Wilson, 1913–1921

33 *The American Elm Tree on the North Lawn of the White House*

The 2013 White House Christmas Ornament honors President Woodrow Wilson and his quest for lasting world peace by featuring the American Elm he planted on the White House North Lawn in December 1913, just before Christmas, to signify hope. The image shows the elm on a wintry day surrounded by a wreath of elm leaves, olive branches, and holly, and a red ribbon featuring Wilson's monogram. Two peace doves perch on the olive branches. The reverse of the ornament is inscribed with a facsimile of Wilson's signature and the words he delivered in his War Message to Congress of April 2, 1917: "Peace must be planted upon the tested foundations of political liberty."

Woodrow Wilson, born in Virginia, was first a scholar, with a doctorate in political science and history. He taught at Princeton University, led the university as president, and then was elected governor of New Jersey. In 1913 he moved into the White House with Ellen Wilson, a talented artist of the Impressionist style. Before her illness, she organized White House weddings for two of the three Wilson daughters. During these years the Wilson administration was notable for establishing the Federal Reserve, championing labor laws, and launching the National Park Service.

President Wilson's two terms in office are defined by the devastation of World War I, yet he is remembered for his resolve that the Great War would truly end all wars. The conflict began in Europe in August 1914, and even as Wilson proclaimed U.S. neutrality, his wife, Ellen Axson Wilson, lay dying in the White House. Two years later Wilson was happily remarried and reelected on the slogan "He Kept Us Out of War," but it was soon apparent that Germany's submarine attacks on neutral shipping could not be ignored. In April 1917 Congress declared war. In early 1918 Wilson set forth his "Fourteen Points" as a plan for "peace without victory." It proposed an international organization for maintaining peace, and Wilson's vision of a League of Nations was written into the peace treaty. In 1919 Wilson was awarded the Nobel Peace Prize.

MEASURING 2¾ INCHES IN DIAMETER AND ½ INCH IN DEPTH, THIS TWO-SIDED ORNAMENT FEATURES AN ACRYLIC DOME OVER A TINTED IMAGE, SURROUNDED BY A 24K GOLD-FINISHED BRASS WREATH WITH ENAMEL COLORS.

34 *The Presidential Special on*
"The Voyage of Understanding"

The 2014 White House Christmas Ornament honors President Warren G. Harding by commemorating his "Voyage of Understanding" with a two-piece miniature replica of the Presidential Special. One piece is designed after a steam-powered locomotive attached to the coal car that would have fueled it, and the other is the *Superb*, the president's private heavyweight Pullman car. The two replicas can be hung as two separate ornaments or linked together.

As a young boy, Warren G. Harding dreamed of being a locomotive engineer. This wish came true for 51 minutes when, as president, he took over the controls on the Alaskan Railroad during his "Voyage of Understanding," a transcontinental speaking and sightseeing tour. The last car on the Presidential Special, named *Superb*, was outfitted with a platform and public address system from which President Harding made appearances and delivered speeches at stops across the country. The last-known photograph of President Harding is of him on the *Superb* shortly before his death in San Francisco on August 2, 1923. The next day President Harding's casket was placed on board the *Superb* to begin a return trip to Washington, D.C., during which an estimated 3 million people paid their last respects.

Warren G. Harding had been a newspaperman in Ohio before entering politics. As editor and publisher of the *Marion Star*, he made political friends and useful connections, and he polished his speaking skills. He served in the state senate and then the U.S. Senate on his way to the presidency. Promising "the resumption of our onward, normal way," he raised tariffs and reduced taxes on corporations. Although his "normal way" also meant not making overseas commitments, he did work to improve relations with the nations of North and South America and to reduce the number of warships and other naval armaments. He also advocated for U.S. membership in the World Court.

THIS THREE-DIMENSIONAL 24K GOLD-FINISHED BRASS AND COLORED ENAMEL ORNAMENT IS COMPRISED OF TWO PIECES THAT CAN BE LINKED TOGETHER: AN ENGINE MEASURING ¾ x 3¼ x ½ INCHES AND A PULLMAN CAR MEASURING ¾ x 3¼ x ½ INCHES.

2015
President Calvin Coolidge, 1923–1929

35 *The National Christmas Tree*

The 2015 White House Christmas Ornament honors President Calvin Coolidge with a depiction of the National Christmas Tree illuminated from within and hung with ornaments representing events in his life and presidency. The house and general store represent his birthplace. His favorite hobbies are symbolized by the baseball, fishing basket, and cowboy hat. The kerosene lamp recalls Coolidge's swearing-in ceremony. The microphone marks the first presidential radio address broadcast in December 1923. Near the bottom of the tree are a 1924 presidential campaign button and the Coolidges' pet raccoon. The eagle feathers signify the Indian Citizenship Act signed into law in 1924. The Distinguished Flying Cross notes the honor bestowed on Charles Lindbergh in 1927. The sketch of Mount Rushmore is for the dedication ceremony in 1927. The socks at the bottom right suggest the wit of the president who once gave his wife Grace a basket of socks to mend. When she asked him if he had married her to darn his socks, he replied, "No—but I find it mighty handy."

In the early morning of August 3, 1923, Vice President Coolidge was in Vermont visiting his father, far from telephones and electricity, when he received a telegram announcing President Warren G. Harding's sudden death. Coolidge's father, a notary public, administered the Oath of Office to his son in the family sitting room at 2:47 a.m. by the light of a kerosene lamp. Though Coolidge had risen to political prominence as governor of Massachusetts, he cultivated his public image as a frugal and reticent Vermonter with a reputation for integrity. As president he cut taxes and vetoed federal spending legislation.

Inside the White House, the Coolidges celebrated that next Christmas quietly with their teenage sons, but outside, on the Ellipse, the president made history by pushing a button to illuminate more than 2,500 lights on the first National Christmas Tree, a 60-foot fir from Vermont. Choirs sang carols, and the U.S. Marine Band played Christmas music. Coolidge's tree-lighting ceremony was the first of what is now the annual Pageant of Peace.

ILLUMINATED FROM WITHIN BY LED LIGHTS AND MEASURING 4 x 2 x ½ INCHES, THIS THREE-DIMENSIONAL ORNAMENT IS MADE OF 24K GOLD-FINISHED BRASS WITH ENAMEL COLORS.

White House Christmas 2015

COOLIDGE AND DAWES

2016
President Herbert Hoover, 1929–1933

36   *The Christmas Eve Fire of 1929*

The 2016 White House Christmas Ornament honors President Herbert Hoover with a three-dimensional depiction of the fire engine that responded to a 1929 Christmas Eve fire at the White House. It carries a Christmas tree in its truck-bed and is decorated with a holiday wreath on its front grille. The next year the Hoovers gave children toy fire engine trucks like this as Christmas gifts.

The White House was filled with Christmas cheer when the traditional festivities got under way on the evening of December 24, 1929. The president and his wife Lou were entertaining his staff and their children at a Christmas party while the U.S. Marine Band played carols in the Entrance Hall. Then the chief usher whispered urgently in the president's ear: "The executive office is on fire!" Built in 1902, the wing contained the president's offices, including the first Oval Office, added in 1909. Hoover and his son left immediately, to rescue as many of the president's papers as time allowed, while the first lady calmly remained to supervise the party. The band played on. Even though some of the hoses froze and created geysers of ice, the fire was extinguished by about 10:30 p.m. The exterior walls had survived, but the roof, attic, and floors had to be rebuilt. In April 1930 Hoover and his aides moved back into the remodeled West Wing.

Herbert Hoover of Iowa was the first president from west of the Mississippi. Trained as a mining engineer, he made a fortune, then began a career in public service. During World War I he headed relief for Belgium and later ran the U.S. Food Administration with efficiency. With his reputation as a humanitarian, he seemed well prepared for the presidency, but six months after his inauguration the stock market crashed and the long Great Depression began. Hoover's reliance on volunteerism and community generosity were not enough to stop the suffering: the factory closings and farm foreclosures, the bank failures and breadlines, the loss of income and the rise in unemployment.

MEASURING 1¾ X 4¼ X ¾ INCHES, THIS THREE-DIMENSIONAL ORNAMENT IS MADE OF 24K GOLD-FINISHED BRASS WITH A NICKEL COATING AND ENAMEL COLORS.

37   *The Bald Eagle Inaugural Cartouche*

The 2017 White House Christmas Ornament honors President Franklin D. Roosevelt with his monogram and a depiction of the bald eagle used to decorate the podium of his first inauguration in 1933, the last presidential inauguration held in March. Three inaugurations lay ahead for him, but they would be held on January 20, as mandated by an amendment to the Constitution. On the reverse of the ornament is an image of the South Front of the White House above a small Christmas tree that is capturing the attention of Roosevelt's beloved Scottish terrier, Fala.

Franklin D. Roosevelt took office during the Great Depression. Americans had given him a landslide victory, hoping for rescue from economic turmoil. And the president delivered. His domestic recovery programs began immediately and he persevered through criticism to ease the worst aspects of the Depression, initiating a slow but effective climb toward recovery. But he would face a second crisis: World War II. After Pearl Harbor he was commander in chief of troops in action around the world. Victory was imminent when he died in April 1945. Through it all, President Roosevelt gave hope to Americans, who elected him president an unprecedented four times.

Franklin Delano Roosevelt, fifth cousin of Theodore Roosevelt, had seemed destined for greatness. He was a New York state senator and assistant secretary of the navy, but personal tragedy followed when he was struck with poliomyelitis. Though he never walked on his own again, he returned to politics. As governor of New York, he addressed economic challenges with the public relief programs that won him the presidency. Always he was supported by his wife, Eleanor Roosevelt, a fifth cousin once removed. Their White House was crowded with family, staff, and guests, the most famous being Winston Churchill, prime minister of Britain. In 1941, shortly after the attack on Pearl Harbor, Churchill stood with the president on the South Portico and watched the lighting of the National Christmas Tree.

MEASURING 3¼ x 3 x ½ INCHES, THIS GOLD-FINISHED BRASS, TWO-SIDED ORNAMENT FEATURES A NICKEL COATING AND ENAMEL COLORS.

38 *The Truman Balcony*

The 2018 White House Christmas Ornament honors President Harry S. Truman with a design that features the Truman Balcony on one side and a Christmas tree in his renovated Blue Room on the other. The seal on top of the ornament depicts Truman's personal redesign of the Presidential Seal. Exemplifying his wish for peace in the aftermath of World War II, he turned the eagle's head from left to right, away from the cluster of arrows in its talons, and toward the olive branch of peace.

Vice President Harry S. Truman of Missouri came to the presidency in the shadow of President Franklin D. Roosevelt but emerged with a stature of his own. Few presidents faced the challenges that awaited him. The most destructive war in world history was about to end in Europe, and to hasten its end in the Pacific, Truman approved the use of the atomic bomb. Then he began an unprecedented program for rebuilding the nations of war-torn former enemies. Truman oversaw the founding of the United Nations to keep the peace but built the North Atlantic Treaty Organization for mutual defense as Cold War tensions with the Soviet Union rose. In 1950 he sent U.S. troops to South Korea in support of a UN effort to stop communist North Korea's aggression.

Living in the White House, Truman noticed swaying chandeliers and cracked plaster, and when the leg of his daughter's grand piano broke through the floor, he moved out, across the street to Blair House. In a massive three-year renovation the interior of the mansion was gutted and rebuilt, but Truman insisted that the original stone walls, which had survived the fire of 1814, be saved. When he moved back in, the house looked the same, the rooms arranged as always, but with every modern convenience, now supported by steel and concrete. One change he had made before the renovation was now permanent. His Second Floor balcony installed within the South Front Portico had been controversial, but it has ever since been a favorite retreat for first families and their guests.

THIS TWO-SIDED, THREE-DIMEN-
SIONAL ORNAMENT FEATURES A
2½ x 2¼ x ¾ INCH SOUTH PORTICO
AND A ¾ INCH DIAMETER 24K
GOLD-FINISHED BRASS PRESIDEN-
TIAL SEAL WITH ENAMEL COLORS.

The White House   Christmas 2018

39 *The First Presidential Helicopter*

The 2019 White House Christmas Ornament honors President Dwight D. Eisenhower with a representation of his presidential helicopter. One side features the Presidential Seal, representing Eisenhower's two terms in office as commander in chief. On the other is his five-star rank, honoring his military service as a general in the U.S. Army.

Born in Texas and raised in Kansas, Dwight D. Eisenhower began his army career at West Point. Recognized for his strong executive ability, he rose steadily through the ranks. His commanding role in World War II, especially his planning of the climactic Normandy invasion on D-Day, made it almost inevitable that he run for president. The electorate expected greatness from him. The war had been over for nearly eight years when he was inaugurated, but conflict had flared in a divided Korea. There he shortly secured an armistice, yet his entire presidency was marked by the menace of tensions between the democratic West and the Communist East, and specifically between the superpowers, the United States and the Soviet Union. This Cold War was intensified by nuclear threats, and the arduous standoff lasted long after his administration.

Throughout his army career and his presidency, Eisenhower proved to be an innovator. He was the first president to fly in a helicopter while in office, and he used helicopters frequently to commute short distances, beginning a form of presidential transportation that remains essential today. Increasingly aware of his role as a calming presence for the public, and the power of his famous grin, he turned to television. At the White House he had the Broadcast Room, designed for radio communication, adapted for television, and he addressed the nation at critical moments, as when he sent U.S. troops to Little Rock, to protect nine African American students in the desegregation of the city's Central High School. At the end of his presidency he addressed the nation again, in a farewell that warned against the influence of the "the military-industrial complex."

MEASURING 1¼ x 4½ x ¾ INCHES WITH BLADES EXTENDING 4¼ INCHES, THIS THREE DIMENSIONAL ORNAMENT IS MADE OF 24K GOLD-FINISHED BRASS WITH ENAMEL COLORS.

President John F. Kennedy, 1961–1963

40 *President Kennedy's Posthumous Portrait*

The 2020 White House Christmas Ornament honors President John F. Kennedy with a depiction of his posthumous official White House portrait, made in 1970 by Aaron Shikler, the artist selected by the president's widow, Jacqueline Kennedy. The president is shown deep in thought, with his head bowed, reminding the viewer of the tragedy of his unfinished presidency. After she left the White House in 1963, Mrs Kennedy returned only once, in 1971, to view this portrait with her children.

John F. Kennedy of Massachusetts was just 43 when he took office. Although his vibrant presidency was cut short by an assassin's bullet in November 1963, his legacy lives on in his youthful belief in America and his faith in America's responsibilities to the world. Not six weeks into his administration he established the Peace Corps, inspiring thousands of Americans to take assignments in developing nations, teaching and providing technical assistance. He reinvigorated America's space program and promoted legislation that would protect African American rights. And he faced the most serious crisis of the Cold War era in 1962, when the Soviets began to install missile sites in Cuba. Kennedy's combination of a show of force with behind-the scenes communications resolved the standoff, the closest the superpowers ever came to nuclear war. In the aftermath, he secured a nuclear test ban treaty.

In the White House the Kennedy administration is remembered for its elegant cultural events. First Lady Jacqueline Kennedy, especially, worked to restore the historic decor of the State Rooms and furnish them with antiques, including original pieces donated back to the White House. She wanted the White House to be a repository for American fine and decorative arts and pushed Congress for legislation that made its furnishings a permanent collection. To enhance the public's understanding, appreciation, and enjoyment of the White House, she established the White House Historical Association. But the Kennedys are also remembered for their two young children, who certainly did enjoy the White House, romping with their father in the Oval Office and playing with their pony on the White House Lawn.

MEASURING 3 x 3 ¾ INCHES THIS ORNAMENT IS MADE OF 24K GOLD-FINISHED BRASS WITH ENAMEL COLORS.

2021
President Lyndon Baines Johnson, 1963–1969

41 *Blue Room Christmas Tree*

The 2021 White House Christmas Ornament honors President Lyndon Baines Johnson with a painting of the Blue Room Christmas tree by Robert H. Laessig that was featured on the Johnsons' 1967 Christmas card. On the reverse of the ornament is a quote from President Johnson's address to a joint session of Congress in 1965 with which he calls on legislators to support a bill that would protect the right to vote. The quote reads, "Our mission is at once the oldest and the most basic of this country: to right wrong, to do justice, to serve man." Encircling the quote are bluebonnet flowers, the state flower of Texas, inspired by Lady Bird Johnson's beautification programs.

On November 22, 1963, following the assassination of President John F. Kennedy, Vice President Lyndon Baines Johnson took the Oath of Office aboard *Air Force One* in his home state of Texas. As president, Johnson focused on healing the mourning nation and honoring his predecessor by adopting Kennedy's objectives. President Johnson felt there could be no better way to do this than to pass the Civil Rights Act, which he signed into law on July 2, 1964. He also carried on the legacy of President and Mrs. Kennedy's support of the arts and humanities by helping to establish the National Endowment for the Humanities and the National Endowment for the Arts. And he signed the Public Broadcasting Act that later led to the creation of the Public Broadcasting Service (PBS) and National Public Radio (NPR).

For their first Christmases as a first family, the Johnsons traveled to the LBJ Ranch in Stonewall, Texas, but in 1967 they decided to stay in Washington, D.C., with their expanding family that would include two grandchildren by the following Christmas. Beginning in 1964, the Johnsons' Christmas card had been designed by Robert Laessig of American Greetings to feature, at Lady Bird Johnson's request, historic trees planted by previous presidents. In 1967, however, in another departure from their traditions, Mrs. Johnson requested that the card feature the Christmas tree in the Blue Room. The message inside the card commemorated the first White House Christmas tree introduced in 1889 by President Benjamin Harrison and displayed in the Yellow Oval Room on the Second Floor of the White House.

MEASURING 3 x 3 INCHES THIS ORNAMENT IS MADE OF 24K GOLD-PLATED BRASS WITH ENAMEL COLORS.